buy Authority To Heal

LEADER'S GUIDE

AUTHORITY
to
HEAL

D0814074

LEADER'S GUIDE

AUTHORITY
to
HEAL

RESTORING THE LOST INHERITANCE OF
God's Healing Power

RANDY CLARK

DESTINY IMAGE® PUBLISHERS, INC.

P.O. Box 310, Shippensburg, PA 17257-0310

"Promoting Inspired Lives."

This book and all other Destiny Image and Destiny Image Fiction books are available at Christian bookstores and distributors worldwide.

Cover design by Eileen Rockwell

Interior design by Terry Clifton

For more information on foreign distributors, call 717-532-3040.

Or reach us on the Internet: www.destinyimage.com

ISBN 13: TP 978-0-7684-0892-8

For Worldwide Distribution, Printed in the U.S.A.

2 3 4 5 6 7 8 9 10 11 /20 19 18

SESSIONS

HOW TO USE THIS LEADER'S GUIDE

The Authority to Heal Study Guide is divided into eight video sessions and includes 40 days of reinforcement devotionals. This Leader's Guide is designed to help group leaders effectively facilitate the group study of *Authority to Heal* in a variety of settings.

Each week, group leaders should be prepared to do the following:

1. Preview the group session (DVD segment). We recommend leaders watch the group sessions first to familiarize yourself with the material before presenting it to a group or class.

2. Be comfortable with the format. Each *Authority to Heal* session will consist of the following:

   a. **Summary of the weekly session.** This summary gives a brief overview of the session and the topics to be covered by Randy.

b. **Discussion Questions for group/class/ individual discussion and reflection.** Review the discussion questions in advance in order to better help the group/class respond and answer any questions that might arise.

c. **Group Activation Exercise:** Review the instructions to familiarize yourself with the activity. After participants watch the session, take notes, and engage in discussion, help them put the teachings into practice through the Group Activation Exercise.

3. Encourage group members to keep up with their daily study guide exercises. These daily activities are designed to reinforce the material learned during the Group Sessions, and consist of the following:

a. **Devotional reading:** Each daily devotional segment offers an outlet for increased clarification of and meditation on the week's topic.

b. **Reflection questions:** These questions are designed to help participants critically interact with the material introduced in the sessions.

c. **Prayer directive:** Each prayer directive introduces a short, simple prayer topic that helps give voice to the empowering work of the Holy Spirit in the life of participants and enables students to understand that healing ministry begins in the place of prayer.

BASIC LEADER GUIDELINES

The goal of this study is to help facilitate spiritual transformation in the participants. With that in mind, each session is sequenced to take participants from information to transformation. There are several ways you can accomplish this. We encourage you to begin by seeking the Lord's direction and the creativity of the Holy Spirit, keeping in mind that our suggested guidelines are just that—guidelines. They are not meant to be comprehensive, but rather to augment what the Lord will direct you to as you move through this study.

Spiritual formation in a group setting has an organic Holy Spirit nature that is uniquely designed by God to enable Him to interact with participants on a personal level, and you, the group leader are there to facilitate what God is doing. Enjoy the journey and encourage participants to do the same. What follows are some suggestions as to how you can use this curriculum.

CHURCH SMALL GROUP

Often, Churches feature a variety of different small group opportunities per season, in terms of books, curriculum resources, and Bible studies. *Authority to Heal* can be included among the offering of titles for whatever season you are launching for your particular small group program.

It is recommended that you have a minimum of four to five people, and a maximum of 12 people for a small group. If you have more than 12 enrolled, either break the group into multiple groups, or consider moving toward a Church class model, which will be outlined next.

Here are the essentials for a small group setting:

- *Meeting place*: Either the leader's home, or a space provided by the Church.

- *Appropriate technology:* A DVD player attached to a TV that is large enough for all of the group members to see (and loud enough for everyone to hear).

- *Leader/Facilitator*: This person will often be the host if the small group is being conducted at someone's home; but it can also be a team. The leader(s) will direct the session from beginning to end, which includes sending out weekly reminder e-mails to participants and closing out the sessions in prayer before dismissing the group. It is helpful for leaders to select certain people in the group to assist with various elements of the meeting such as worship, prayer, ministry time, etc. In this way leaders do not become overburdened and participants are drawn into the life of the group.

Sample Schedule for a 7:00 P.M. Home Group Meeting

This sample schedule incorporates all elements—from the extremely practical (such as serving refreshments) to the spiritual (facilitating the question/answer time).

- Before arrival: Ensure that refreshments are on site approximately 45 minutes before the meeting. If they need to be refrigerated, ensure they are preserved appropriately until 15 minutes prior to the official meeting time.

- 6:15 P.M.: Leaders arrive at meeting home or facility.

- 6:15–6:25 P.M.: Connect with hosts, co-hosts, and/or co-leaders to review the evening's program.

- 6:25–6:35 P.M.: Pray with hosts, co-hosts, and/ or co-leaders for the evening's events. Here are some sample prayer directives:

  - For the video sessions to connect with and transform all who hear it.

  - For dialogue and conversation that edifies.

  - For comfort and transparency among group members.

- 6:35–6:45: Ensure technology is functioning properly!

- Test the DVDs featuring the teaching sessions, making sure they are set up to the appropriate session.

- 6:45–7:00 P.M.: Welcome and greet participants.

- 7:00–7:10 P.M.: Fellowship, community, and refreshments.

- 7:10–7:12 P.M.: Gather everyone together in the meeting place.

- 7:12–7:30 P.M.: Introductory prayer/ice-breaker.

- 7:30–7:40 P.M.: Ministry and prayer time.

- 7:40–8:10 P.M.: Watch DVD session.

- 8:10–8:35 P.M.: Discuss DVD session.

- 8:35–9:00 P.M.: Empower activity, closing and final prayer.

This sample scheduled is *not* intended to lock you into a formula. It is simply provided as a template to help you get started. Our hope is that you would customize it according to the unique needs of your group.

CHURCH CLASS | MID-WEEK CLASS | SUNDAY SCHOOL CURRICULUM

Churches of all sizes offer a variety of classes purposed to develop members into more effective disciples of Jesus. *Authority to Heal* is an invaluable addition to a Church's class offering, providing adults of all ages the opportunity to start operating in God's supernatural healing power.

INDIVIDUAL STUDY

While this study is designed for use in a group or class setting, it also works as a tool that can equip any individual participant through self-guided study.

STEPS TO LAUNCHING AN *AUTHORITY TO HEAL* GROUP OR CLASS

PREPARE WITH PRAYER!

1. *Pray!* If you are a **Church leader**, prayerfully consider how *Authority to Heal* could transform the culture and climate of your Church community.

2. If you are a **group leader** or **class facilitator**, pray for those who will be attending your group or signing up for your class.

PREPARE PRACTICALLY!

Determine how you will be using the Authority to Heal curriculum.

Identify which of the following formats you will be using the curriculum in:

- Church-sponsored small group study.

- Church class (Wednesday night, Sunday morning, etc.).

- Individual study.

Determine a meeting location and ensure availability of appropriate equipment.

Keep in mind the number of people who may attend. You will also need AV (audiovisual) equipment. The more comfortable the setting, the more people will enjoy being there and spending time ministering to each other!

Just a word of caution here: the larger the group, the greater your need for co-leaders or assistants. The ideal small group size is difficult to judge; however, once you get more than 10-12 people, it becomes difficult for each member to feel "heard." If your group is larger than 12 people, consider either having two or more small group discussion leaders, or "multiplying" the larger group into two smaller ones.

Determine the format for your meetings.

By determining what kind of meeting you will be hosting, you become better equipped to develop an appropriate schedule for the meeting, identify potential co-leaders, and order the appropriate quantity of resources.

Set a schedule for your meetings.

Once you have established the format for your meetings, set a schedule for your meetings. Some groups like to have a time of fellowship or socializing, either before or after the meeting begins, where light refreshments are offered. Some groups will want to incorporate times of worship and personal ministry into the small group or class.

Establish a start date along with a weekly meeting day and time.

This eight-week curriculum should be followed consistently and consecutively. Be mindful of the fact that while there are eight weeks of material, most groups will want to meet one last time after completing the last week, to celebrate in a purely social setting such as going out to dinner together, seeing a movie, or something similar. This is very normal and should be encouraged to continue the community momentum that the small group experience initiates. Another possibility that will extend the number of times you meet is to designate the first meeting as a time to get to know each other and "break the ice" without actually beginning to work through the material. This can be facilitated with light snacks or a simple meal.

Look far enough ahead on the calendar to account for anything that might interfere. Choose a day that works well for the members of your group. For a Church class, be sure to coordinate the time with the appropriate ministry leader.

Advertise!

Getting the word out in multiple ways is most effective. Print up flyers, post a sign-up sheet, make an announcement in Church services or group meetings, send out weekly e-mails and text messages, set up your own blog or website, or post the event on the social media avenue you and your group utilize most (Facebook, Twitter, etc.). A personal invitation or phone call is a great way to reach those who might need that little bit of extra encouragement.

For any type of small group or class to succeed, it must be endorsed by and encouraged from the leadership. For larger Churches with multiple group/class offerings, it is wise to provide Church members with literature featuring all of the different small group/class options. This information should also be featured online in an easily accessible page on your Church website.

For smaller Churches, it is a good idea for the pastor or a key leader to announce the launch of a small group course or class from the pulpit during an announcement time.

Gather your materials.

Leaders: you will need the *Authority to Heal Curriculum Kit*, which includes this Leader's Guide, the Study Guide, the DVDs, and the *Authority to Heal* book. Although the study can be done without the book it is not advisable since the principles in the book are absolutely essential to what participants will be learning during the eight-week curriculum. The Session Summary for each week includes a weekly reading assignment from the book. It is recommended that participants read these segments of the book weekly along with completing their weekly study guide readings and exercises.

Participants: each participant will need a personal copy of the *Authority to Heal* Study Guide, and the *Authority to Heal* book.

We recommend that all materials be purchased at one time. This will ensure that each participant will have the materials they need from the start. Also, many booksellers and distributors offer discounts on multiple orders, saving everyone money.

STEP FORWARD!

- Arrive at your meeting location in *plenty* of time to prepare; frazzled last-minute preparations do not put you in a place of rest, and your group members will sense your stress! Ensure that all AV equipment is working properly, and that you have ample supplies for each member. Nametags are a great idea, at least for the first couple of meetings. Icebreaker and introduction activities are also a good idea for the first meeting.

- Pray for your members. As much as possible, make yourself available to them. You may also need to encourage those who struggle, grow weary, or lose heart. Make sure your members stay committed so they experience the full benefits of this study.

- Multiply yourself. Is there someone you know who was not able to attend your group? Help them to initiate their own small group now that you know how effective *Authority to Heal* can be in a group setting!

LEADER CHECKLIST

ONE TO TWO MONTHS PRIOR

__ Have you determined a start date for your class or small group?

__ Have you determined the format, meeting day and time, and weekly meeting schedule?

__ Have you selected a meeting location (making sure you have adequate space and AV equipment available)?

__ Have you advertised? Do you have a sign-up sheet to ensure you order enough materials?

TWO WEEKS TO ONE MONTH PRIOR

__ Have your ordered materials? You will need a copy of the *Authority to Heal curriculum*, along with copies of the study guide and book for each participant.

__ Have you organized your meeting schedule/format?

ONE TO TWO WEEKS PRIOR

__ Have you received all your materials?

__ Have you reviewed the DVDs and your leader's guide to familiarize yourself with the material and to ensure everything is in order?

__ Have you planned and organized your refreshments, if you are planning to provide them? Some leaders will handle this themselves and some find it easier to allow participants to sign up to provide refreshments if they would like to do so.

__ Have you advertised and promoted? This includes sending out e-mails to all participants, setting up a Facebook group, setting up a group through your Church's database system (if available), promotion in the Church bulletin, etc.

__ Have you appointed co-leaders to assist you with the various portions of the group/class?

FIRST MEETING DAY

Plan to arrive *early!* Give yourself extra time to set up the meeting space, double-check all AV equipment and organize your materials. It might be helpful to ask participants to arrive 15 minutes early for the first meeting to allow for distribution of materials and any icebreaker activity you might have planned.

SESSION DISCUSSION QUESTIONS:
WEEKLY OVERVIEW OF MEETINGS/ GROUP SESSIONS

WELCOME AND FELLOWSHIP TIME (10-15 MINUTES)

This usually begins five to ten minutes prior to the designated meeting time and typically continues up until ten minutes after the official starting time. Community is important. One of the issues for many small group/class environments is the lack of connectivity. People walk around inspired and resourced, but they remain disconnected from other believers. Foster an environment where community is welcome but, at the same time, not distracting. This tends to be a problem that plagues small group settings more than classes.

Welcome everyone as they walk in. If it is a small group environment, as the host or leader, be intentional about connecting with each person as they enter the meeting space. If it is a classroom environment, it is still recommended that the leader connect with each participant. However, there will be less pressure for the participants to feel connected immediately in a traditional class setting versus a more intimate, small group environment.

Refreshments and **materials.** Refreshments are always a welcome sight and help facilitate fellowship between group members.

In a class setting, talk with participants and ensure that they have purchased all of their necessary materials (*Authority to Heal* Study Guide and a copy of the *Authority to Heal* book). Ideally, the participants will have received their resources prior to Week 1, but if not, ensure that the materials are present at the meeting and available for group members to pick up/purchase. It is advisable that you have several copies of the study guide and book available at the small group meeting just in case people did not pick up their copies at the designated time.

Call the meeting to order. This involves gathering everyone together in the appropriate place and clearly stating that the meeting is getting ready to start.

Pray! Open every session in prayer, specifically addressing the topic that you will be covering in the upcoming meeting time.

INTRODUCTIONS
(10 MINUTES—FIRST CLASS ONLY)

While a time of formal introduction should only be done on the first week of the class/session, it is recommended that in subsequent meetings, especially those in larger Church setting, to have participants state their name when addressing a question, making a prayer request, giving a comment, etc. If you are conducting this study in a small group setting you will discontinue this practice once everyone gets to know each other. Short icebreaker activities are always helpful in the first week or two but not necessary once the group has gelled.

- **(First Meeting) Introduce** yourself and allow each participant to briefly introduce himself or herself. This should work fine for both small group and class environments. In a small group, you can go around the room and have each person introduce him or herself one at a time. In a classroom setting, establish some type of flow and then have each person give a quick introduction (name, interesting factoid, etc.).

- **(First Meeting) Discuss** the schedule for the meetings. Provide participants an overview of what the next eight weeks will look like. If you plan to do any type of social activities, you might want to advertise those right up front, noting that while the curriculum officially runs for eight weeks, there will be a ninth week dedicated to fellowship and some type of fun activity if this is what you decide to do.

- **(First Meeting) Distribute** materials to each participant. Briefly orient the participants to the book and study guide, explaining the 20-25 minute time commitment for each day. Encourage each person to engage fully in this journey—they will get out of it only as much as they invest. The purpose for the daily reinforce-ment activities is *not* to add busy work to their lives. The time of day they do the activities is not important, just that they do them. Encour-age people to do whatever works best for their schedule.

PRAYER/MINISTRY TIME (5-15 MINUTES)

At this point, you can transition from the welcome into a time of prayer.

It is recommended that this initial time of prayer be five to ten minutes in length; but if the group is made up of people who do not mind praying longer, than it should not be discouraged. The key is stewarding everyone's time well while maintaining focus on the most important things.

Prayer should be navigated carefully, as there will always be people who use it as an opportunity to speak longer than they ought, complain about circumstances in their lives, or potentially even gossip about other people.

If you feel it would be appropriate to integrate a praise and worship component as well, that is certainly recommended. Often, a time of worship is conducive to creating an environment where the Holy Spirit's presence and power are welcomed.

TRANSITION TIME

At this point, you will transition from prayer/ministry time to watching the *Authority to Heal* DVD session.

Group leaders/class teachers: It is recommended that you have the DVD in the player and set to the appropriate session so that all you have to do is press "PLAY" when it's time to watch the video.

VIDEO/TEACHING (20-60 MINUTES)

Some of the *Authority to Heal* video sessions will be lengthier than others. Use discretion. This is why it is important for you to preview the week's session beforehand. Once you determine how long the actual video session will be, you can plan how long you will focus on the other aspects of the meeting (prayer, praise and worship, discussion questions, etc.).

Encourage participants to take notes during the video sessions. Ideally, they can take notes in the study guide itself, but if they prefer, they can also keep a journal that is specific to the *Authority to Heal* study.

DISCUSSION QUESTIONS (15-30 MINUTES, DEPENDING ON HOW LONG THE VIDEO SESSION WAS)

In the leader's guide, each question will look like the following (see example below from Week 1):

1. Read Matthew 11:12. What does it look like to *forcefully* or *violently* lay hold of God's Kingdom?

2. What do you think it looks like for God to "show Himself strong" through you (see 2 Chron. 16:9)?

3. What do you currently believe about God's healing power?

    a. He healed in the past during biblical times, but He does not heal anymore.

    b. He still heals, but we should not expect it to be normal.

4. Why do you think so many Christians have a difficult time embracing their role in healing ministry?

Some lessons will have more questions than others. Also, there might be some instances where you choose to cut certain questions out for the sake of time. This is entirely up to you, and in a circumstance where the Holy Spirit is moving and appears to be focusing on some questions more than others, flow in sync with the Holy Spirit. He will not steer you wrong!

ACTIVATION EXERCISE

After the group discussion questions, take 15-20 minutes for an interactive activation exercise, where individuals have the opportunity to interact with what they just learned.

You may wish to provide paper and pens for these exercises.

DAILY EXERCISES

Remind participants of the daily exercises in their study guide. Encourage everyone to participate fully in this journey in order to get the most out of it. The daily exercises should not take more than five-ten minutes—however, encourage participants to interact with the daily prompts and, if time permits, make their study time between 15 and 20 minutes in order to get the most out of the material.

Be sure to let participants know if the meeting location will change or differ from week to week, or if there are any other pertinent announcements for your group/class. Weekly e-mails, Facebook updates, and text messages are great tools to communicate with your group. If your Church has a data-base tool that allows for communication between small group/class leaders and members, that works exceptionally well.

ALWAYS AIM TO CLOSE EACH MEETING IN PRAYER.

Session 1

MARKED BY HIS POWER

*Just as the early disciples received
the empowering of the Holy Spirit
and ministered powerfully in
the name of Jesus, you can too.*

*God is inviting you into the
supernatural lifestyle that He
intends for all believers.*

*In the last days, God says, I will pour
out my Spirit on all people.*
—Acts 2:17

SESSION 1 SUMMARY

From the moment you received Jesus as your Lord and Savior, He has been inviting you into a supernatural lifestyle. When you accept His invitation, it will transform the way you understand what the Christian faith looks like and how we are to function as Christians in the world today. God desires to use you, and He makes His Holy Spirit available to equip you for this task. Living a supernatural lifestyle should be normative for all believers, not something unusual that is relegated to a few. Moving in the gifts of healing, in the authority of the name of Jesus and in the power of the Holy Spirit is one way we carry out the Great Commission. The good news of the gospel of Jesus Christ cannot be advanced through our human endeavors. God's Kingdom advances in His power and authority.

In this session you will have an opportunity to reflect on passages of Scripture that enlighten our understanding of the authority that is available to all believers and to examine what this looks like in your own life. God desires that you and all believers be equipped for the work of ministry so that the Church can operate fully as the empowered body of Jesus Christ in the earth today. So much has been made available to the Church, and we, as believers, should not be willing to settle for less.

DISCUSSION QUESTIONS

1. Read Acts 2. How does the third person of the Trinity—the Holy Spirit—figure in your life?

2. What do you currently believe about the role of the Holy Spirit in the life of the Church and each believer? Why?

3. Why do you think so many Christians don't understand the role of the Holy Spirit in the Christian life?

4. We are living in the time between the book of Acts and the book of Revelation. Are you marked by God's power and authority? What does that statement mean to you?

5. Are you willing to settle *for less* or are you *hungry for more*? Explain.

6. Have willing group/class members briefly share their own experiences of spiritual formation, specifically looking for those who have experienced the power of the Holy Spirit in their life and ministry and how this power and authority has impacted them.

GROUP ACTIVATION EXERCISE

John the Baptist said, "I baptize You with water for repentance. But after me will come one who is more powerful than I, whose sandals I am not fit to carry. He will baptize You with the Holy Spirit and with fire" (Matthew 3:11).

You are invited to embrace the fullness of God's supernatural lifestyle right now, through this prayer for the baptism of the Holy Spirit.

Heavenly Father, I come before You now, thankful that Jesus saved me through His finished work on the cross. I ask that You baptize me now in the Holy Spirit, which I will receive by faith, so that Your power and authority may come upon me, equipping me for Your service. Thank You, Lord Jesus. Amen!

WEEKLY READING ASSIGNMENT

Read the Introduction and Chapters 1 and 2 in *Authority to Heal* and be sure to complete your study guide assignments for this week.

Session 2

FOUNDATIONS FOR DIVINE HEALING

We need look no further than the Bible to see the
biblical basis for the continuation of spiritual gifts, but
in order to do so many must make their way past the
confusion created by the enemy of our souls who labors
tirelessly to keep the Church as powerless as possible.

And as you go, preach, saying, "The Kingdom
of heaven is at hand."Heal the sick, cleanse
the lepers, raise the dead, cast out demons.
Freely you have received, freely give.
—MATTHEW 10:7-8, NKJV

SESSION 2 SUMMARY

Healing flows from the very nature of God. Yahweh-
Rophe healed through Moses and many of His prophets,
who were *types* of Jesus, the Messiah who was to come. Jesus
brought the in-break of the Kingdom of God with its healing power, commissioning all believers to heal the sick. The
Old and New Covenants, the atoning work of Christ on the

cross, and the in-break of the Kingdom of God combine to form the basis for divine healing in the life of the Church.

The enemy has vehemently opposed the contemporary relevance of the gifts of the Spirit necessary for divine healing by throwing many confusing philosophies that are not of God against this truth. In order for the Church as a whole to see the ministry of healing restored, there must be a biblical return to the availability and authority of the supernatural, which includes a theology of healing demonstration and empowerment. God, in His sovereignty has decided to impart the Holy Spirit to His people and use them as conduits to release His power in the earth. It is not a matter of whether or not He wants to heal. God still heals and He wants to heal through you and me. We must learn how to be His conduits. For spiritual gifts to be released and activated in the Church today we must return to the *elementary teaching* of impartation. God has promised another final and radical outpouring among the nations before His Son returns. Again, He will bring it about through His people. Jesus said, "As the Father has sent me, I am sending you" (John 20:21).

desires wholeness

DISCUSSION QUESTIONS

1. In Exodus 15:26 God reveals Himself to His people using the name Yahweh-Rophe, which means "the God who heals." Why do you think healing is so central to the heart of God?

2. Read Hebrews 8:6. The writer of Hebrews says that the New Covenant is "founded on better promises." Among these better promises we

find Romans 8:2-4, which says that through the work of the cross, God's laws now live in our hearts, not on stone tablets, so that—empowered by the Spirit—we can delight in doing God's will. How do you think God intends this New Covenant promise to reflect His nature in the Church today?

3. In First Corinthians 2:1-5 Paul is exhorting the Church in Corinth to not look to the eloquence or intellectual prowess of man as a revelation of God, but to understand that it is in the demonstration of His power that God reveals Himself. Why do you think God uses demonstrations of His power to reveal Himself instead of just words?

4. The New Testament standard for discipleship, as revealed in the parables of Jesus, indicates that the Kingdom of God will inaugurate with power and great growth. If Jesus inaugurated His Kingdom with power and pronounced that it is to experience great growth, how does that translate into the powerless Church we see today?

5. Jesus, God in the flesh, demonstrated great humility during His time on earth, always giving glory to His Father rather than taking it for Himself. We are called to the same humility as ministers of the gospel, but why is humility so often "easier said than done" when it comes to the ministry of healing?

6. Read Acts 19:13-20, the story of some who falsely attempted to heal in the name of Jesus. Who in this story understood the sons of Sceva to be false healers, and what was the end result of this whole episode, and why is this important for us to know?

7. Chapter 6 in *Authority to Heal* clearly lays out the theological foundations for impartation yet the Church today seems to have lost this elementary teaching that was given to us as found in Hebrews 6:1-3. Why is impartation necessary for the advance of the Kingdom?

GROUP ACTIVATION EXERCISE

Break up into small groups of two or three. Using Discussion Question #2, reflect on what it means in your life to delight in doing God's will and reflecting His nature in both the Church and the world today.

WEEKLY READING ASSIGNMENT

Read Chapters 3-6 in *Authority to Heal* and be sure to complete your study guide assignments for this week.

THE ISSUE OF FAITH IN HEALING

God's faith comes from God's grace, and for us
this grace is dependent upon a relationship with
Jesus—abiding in Him. The nature of faith can seem
complex, but the mandate to heal is straightforward.
God is intentional about healing, and He is calling
us to partner with Him with the same intentionality.

*Then the disciples came to Jesus in private
and asked, "Why couldn't we drive it out?" He
replied, "Because you have so little faith. I tell
you the truth, if you have faith as small as a
mustard seed, you can say to this mountain,
'Move from here to there' and it will move.
Nothing will be impossible for you."*
—MATTHEW 17:19-21

SESSION 3 SUMMARY

In order to learn how to flow in God's supernatural
power and authority, we must understand the nature of
faith. Although faith is the key and primary way healing

is received and demonstrated, God is sovereign and able to perform miracles outside of our confines. We must have faith *of* God in order to take hold of—seize—the faith that comes from Him through divine revelation. Our faith can be small but powerful when we believe and receive what God makes available by His grace. God's divine enablement will empower us for the miraculous, coming to us as a situational gift from Him for the moment.

There is a strong connection between healing and faith and the revelatory gifts such as declarations, words of knowledge, prophecy, and teaching. In the same way, there is also a strong connection between hearing and receiving revelation from God that results in faith. All of these revelatory gifts flow out of relationship with Jesus. They are unmerited and happen more often to those who expect them and know how to recognize them. When we teach, especially through testimony, we are laying a foundation that will build faith and an expectation for healing. Our understanding of the nature of faith will enable us to better partner with God in the ministry of healing.

God is intentional about healing, and He will act in ways that express His intentionality. When we learn His ways and study His mighty deeds as found in the Scriptures, we become intimate with Him and are better able to understand what it means to reveal His glory in the ministry of healing. "The promises of God are not a problem to be achieved, but a promise to be received" (Leif Hetland). When we learn to cooperate with the presence of God, ministry moves from laboring and striving to a place of rest and favor.

DISCUSSION QUESTIONS:

1. What is the difference between faith *in* God and faith *of* God, and how does this distinction impact the way in which you understand the nature of faith in terms of operating in the miraculous?

2. What are some of the ways in which we can receive divine revelation? How do you receive divine revelation?

3. How can our faith be small and yet be "mountain-moving faith"?

4. What does it mean to have God's divine enablement empower us as a situational gift for the moment? Have you experienced this?

5. How do you personally recognize revelatory gifts?

6. Revelation 19:10 says that the testimony of Jesus is the spirit of prophecy. What do you understand this verse to mean and why is it important to healing ministry?

7. How do we cooperate with the presence of God in ministry? Share examples from your own ministry times.

GROUP ACTIVATION EXERCISE

To one there is given through the Spirit the message of wisdom, to another the message of knowledge by means of the same Spirit (1 Corinthians 12:8).

Set aside an hour of time for your entire group to meet together. Open in prayer, asking the Lord for words of knowledge. Give everyone about five minutes, encouraging people to write down what they are hearing from God. Invite those who have received words of knowledge to share one of the words they have received. As each person shares, invite those who believe that particular word is for them to stand, and when all words have been given invite those standing to come to the person who spoke that particular word and receive prayer. Allow ample time for prayer. When everyone who wants it has received prayer, invite people to share what God is doing as a result of the word of knowledge and prayer they received.

WEEKLY READING ASSIGNMENT

Reach Chapters 7 and 8 in *Authority to Heal* and be sure to complete your study guide assignments for this week.

Session 4

A HISTORY OF HEALING THEOLOGY AND SUPERNATURAL DEMONSTRATION

There is a difference between confirming the gospel and confirming doctrines and Scripture. A study of the New Testament indicates that the function or purpose of healings and miracles is to be part of the expression of the gospel. The gifts, including healings and miracles, are part of the "good news" of the in-break of the Kingdom of God and are to continue until Jesus' second coming. They display the mercy and love of God as found in Jesus and should never have been separated from His gospel.

For I would not dare say anything except what Christ has accomplished through me to make the Gentiles obedient by word and deed, by the power of miraculous signs and wonders, and by the power of God's Spirit. As a result, I have fully proclaimed the good news about the Messiah from Jerusalem all the way around to Ilyricum.
—ROMANS 15:18-19 HCSB

SESSION 4 SUMMARY

As we look back over the first 400 or more years of Church history, we hear the early fathers collectively saying, "Miracles have not stopped. They still occur today!" So why then do we have such division within the Church today on this issue? How did the Church, which witnessed so much healing its first thousand years, become so closed and skeptical about this vital ministry? I believe we have erred by focusing the redemption we have in Christ almost totally in the future, while making only moral changes available in this present life. This was not the understanding or the focus of the early Church.

The early community of Christians believed in a present power not only for moral change, but also for authority over demons, power over sickness and disease, and the experience of the reality of spiritual gifts in their lives, especially in the corporate life of gathered congregations. Today, we have emptied the Atonement (the cross) of its full effect by an understanding that is correct as far as it goes—substitutionary atonement. Unfortunately, this understanding does not go far enough. It must be balanced by other understandings of the atoning work of Jesus on the cross, especially the *Christus Victor* understanding of atonement. It is only when we understand the fullness of what occurred on the cross that we can fully comprehend all that Jesus did for us in His scourging and crucifixion.

The Anti-Nicene fathers preached a Jesus who cared about releasing captives from demonic influences as well as freeing people from their bondage to sin. In short, they preached the "good news." They preached a Jesus of compassion who cared about the sickness of a man's body as well as his soul. God is much more interested in whether or not we are relationally correct with Him, than in whether or not we have all our doctrinal ducks in a row. Rather than looking at the consequences of sin's curse as the work of the enemy that the Church has the authority and power to come against— to continue the work of Christ who came "to destroy the devil's work" (1 John 3:8)—Christians began to see all things as foreordained and therefore to passively accept what they believed to be God's will. Ultimately, this shift from a warfare worldview to a blueprint worldview would have a distinctly negative impact upon the theology of healing in the Church.

DISCUSSION QUESTIONS

1. For the last 500 years liberal and cessationist Protestant pastors have preached a powerless gospel, teaching North American and European Churches not to believe or expect the gifts of healing and working of miracles in the Church because they no longer exist. How would you refute this liberal and cessationist teaching based on your personal experience?

2. Matthew 4:23 says, "Jesus went about all Galilee, teaching in their synagogues, and preaching the gospel of the Kingdom, and healing all manner of sickness and all manner of disease among the people." When we emphasize the soul without concern for our physical bodies, how does that run contrary to the gospel of Jesus?

3. Read Matthew 8:17: "This was to fulfill what was spoken through the prophet Isaiah: 'He took up our infirmities and carried our diseases.'" Elsewhere in his gospel, Matthew uses the healings of Jesus as proof of His [Jesus'] messianic claims. Do you think God intends the Gospels to be mere history, or is He speaking prophetic testimony through the history of His Church? Why is this important?

4. Read Matthew 4:4 and Second Timothy 3:14-17 and then consider that the age of reason and intellectualism replaced divine revelation and experience with "right reasoning"—if it couldn't be explained by human reasoning, it didn't happen. How does right reasoning run contrary to the nature of Christianity as revelation?

Referencing Matthew 12:29 and Mark 3:27, Randy makes the statement that the energies of God make the power and presence of God tangible today and are the means by which the "strong man's house is plundered." Who is the "strong man" and how do we "plunder his house according to the temptation of Jesus (see Matthew 4; Mark 1:9–13)?

GROUP ACTIVATION EXERCISE

This is what the Lord says, He who made the earth, the Lord who formed it and established it —the Lord is His name: "Call to me and I will answer you and tell you great and unsearchable things you do not know" (Jeremiah 33:2-3).

Using Jeremiah 33:2-3 as your focus, break up into small groups of two or three and share your experiences of Church doctrine regarding divine healing. Then pray and ask God to lead you into greater revelation of His great desire to heal through the finished work of His Son, Jesus.

PRAYER

O Father, open our minds to greater revelations of Your heart of love as expressed in Your matchless Son, Jesus Christ, who stretched out His arms on the cross and gave Himself up for us, for our redemption and healing. May Your truths take root in our hearts so that we can fully embrace all that was accomplished on the cross, and learn to walk in the power and authority given to us in Your precious Holy Spirit. Amen.

WEEKLY READING ASSIGNMENT

Read Chapters 9 and 10 in *Authority to Heal* and be sure and complete your study guide assignments for this week.

Session 5

HOW WE LOST OUR INHERITANCE

The evolution of Christian theology away from the
New Testament emphasis on healing, exorcism and
miracles led to the practice of going so far as to deny
their contemporary occurrence. The result of this is
that now, when it comes to healing miracles, we have
many unbelieving believers, and believing unbelievers

Believe me when I say that I am in the Father
and the Father is in me; or at least believe
on the evidence of the miracles themselves.
—JOHN 14:11

SESSION 5 SUMMARY

The powerful Church of Jesus Christ lost its authority to
serve in power, and its understanding of the gospel as the in-
breaking of the Kingdom of God, abdicating the power and
authority to push back the dominion of the god of this world
through wrong theology regarding the supernatural activity
of God in the world. This evolution of Christian theology
away from the New Testament emphasis on healing and

miracles went so far as to deny their contemporary occurrence. This unbelief springs from a combination of factors from within and outside the Church.

An examination of these factors in the history of the Church, in both Catholicism and Protestantism, is very revealing of the lack of validity of many of the arguments —they are simply not supported by Scripture. Healing has historically been one of the most controversial subjects of the Church, and its restoration in the life of the body of Christ is not without conflict. But God is faithful and not deterred by conflict. His glory shines brightly in the midst of battle. James 1:16-18 says, "Don't be deceived, my dear brothers. Every good and perfect gift is from above, coming down from the Father of the heavenly lights, who does not change like shifting shadows. He chose to give us birth through the Word of truth, that we might be a kind of firstfruits of all He created." God is unchanging and ever faithful, and His supernatural empowerment for the working of miracles and healings in the Church today is evidence. He has unleashed His mighty river of healing on the earth today, making it harder and harder to deny the truth of His Word.

DISCUSSION QUESTIONS

1. The combination of sociological factors highlighted in Chapter 11 contributed to the loss of the Church's supernatural power and authority to heal. What sociological factors do you see today that are impacting the restoration of gifts in the life of the Church?

2. Both Catholicism and Protestantism developed theology that led the Church away from the truth of the Scriptures regarding the operation of the supernatural, with the result that the miraculous works of God today are being labeled by some as myth, legend, and even delusion. Once again the Messiah is fulfilling Isaiah 61, and once again religious authorities are rejecting His testimony. What is your understanding of the Isaiah 61 mandate?

3. Infant baptism has led to a decline of the miraculous in the Church by creating a separation between the baptismal rite and the experience of the Holy Spirit. As a result, many never experience the fullness of the Holy Spirit. What is your baptismal experience, and did it include the experience of the Holy Spirit?

4. The moral corruption of the Middle Ages spilled over into the Church, leading to the Church taking the ministry of healing out of the hands of the laity and placing it in the domain of the clergy, where it has tried to remain. How have you seen this play out in your own Church experience? Do you agree or disagree?

5. Cessationist B.B. Warfield wrote extensively on the cessation of the miraculous in the Church; however, his foundational argument was faulty. After reading Chapter 13, what do you think of Warfield's arguments in light of the scriptural truth that the purpose of miracles is to express

the gospel, not to validate or express correct doctrine?

GROUP ACTIVATION EXERCISE

When Jesus saw Nathanael approaching, He said of him, "Here is a true Israelite, in whom there is nothing false." "How do You know me?" Nathanael asked. Jesus answered, "I saw you while you were still under the fig tree before Philip called you." Then Nathanael declared, "Rabbi, You are the Son of God; You are the King of Israel." Jesus said, "You believe because I told you I saw you under the fig tree. You shall see greater things than that." He then added, "I tell you the truth, you shall see heaven open, and the angels of God ascending and descending on the Son of Man" (John 1:47-51).

Reflecting on John 1:47-51, break up into small groups of two or three and spend time sharing with one another how a word of knowledge profoundly impacted you or someone you know or ministered to. Then, come back together as one large group and have a handful of people share what they shared in their smaller group. With these testimonies as examples, how can cessationism remain a valid argument?

WEEKLY READING ASSIGNMENT

Read Chapters 11, 12, and 13 in *Authority to Heal* and be sure to do your study guide assignments for this week.

Session 6

RECLAIMING OUR AUTHORITY TO HEAL

Can there be any question that the mightiest moves
of the Spirit, which have resulted in the greatest
numbers of people coming to God, have been
those times of revival characterized by powerful
outpourings of spiritual gifts and manifestations of
God's very presence

*In the last days, God says, I will pour out my
Spirit on all people. Your sons and daughters
will prophesy, your young men will see visions,
your old men will dream dreams. Even on my
servants, both men and women, I will pour out
my Spirit in those days, and they will prophesy."*
—Acts 2:17-18

SESSION 6 SUMMARY

When reading the Act 2:17-18 passage, a translation of
the original Greek reveals that Peter's reference to the "last
days" means the days of the Messiah. The dispensation of
the Old Covenant ended with Jesus. We are living in the

days of the New Covenant—the days of the Messiah. In the Old Testament, God dispensed His Spirit in small amounts. In the book of Acts, God's Spirit begins to pour out on all people, Jew and Gentile, and it has not ceased since. This mighty river of God has ebbed and flowed, not due to a lack of God's power, but to the receptivity of those receiving or rejecting it. Today we see an abundance of the gifts of the Spirit pouring out on willing believers resulting in a great increase in the miraculous, especially in the ministry of healing.

Signs of restoration began in the mid-1800s and continue into the twenty-first century. Periods of revival have survived despite the prejudice that still exists in the Church today. Seminaries and Bible colleges that once taught only cessationist liberal doctrine are now beginning to embrace the supernatural move of God that is happening all over the earth today. Classic denominations are seeing their efforts to evangelize eclipsed by Pentecostals who embrace this outpouring of the Holy Spirit's power and the restoration of the power ministries of the Holy Spirit, especially the gifts of healing, working of miracles, and deliverance. Knowledge of the compassionate heart of God is being restored to the Church and to the world it touches. It is nothing short of astounding to discover how significant this move of God, with its recapturing the gifts of the Spirit, is to the growth of the Church.

DISCUSSION QUESTIONS

1. Were you surprised to learn that *The Shantung Revival* by Mary Crawford was reprinted in 1970 with almost all of the phenomena of the

Holy Spirit edited out? How does this make you feel about the validity of Church history that you have been taught over the years?

2. The Second Great Awakening was character-ized by physical manifestations of the Spirit that many found unsettling. Rather than look-ing at the fruit that came from these powerful touches of God on His Church, some chose to label them false and even dangerous. Have you personally experienced physical manifestations as a result of a touch from God or know some-one who has? If so, what was the fruit of these experiences?

3. Randy points out that it is not healthy to allow prejudice to blind us to the reality of the pow-er and authority of God, both historically and in the Church today. Is there any prejudice that is getting in the way of your own experience of God?

4. Many of the great men and women in the his-tory of the Church who were looking for a res-toration of a fully empowered, apostolic Church as seen in the days of the First Pentecost, fo-cused their ministry on the grace, compas-sion and truth of God found in the Bible. How would you like to see knowledge of the com-passion of God restored to the Church today?

5. The doctrine of "Christ is Victor" means that the cross did not just secure our ultimate

salvation but that all of Satan's power was met head-on and defeated, breaking the dominion of the curse. This is the fullness of our salvation. Does the work of the cross stop at substitutionary atonement for you, or does the scope of the cross go beyond? Explain.

GROUP ACTIVATION EXERCISE

"The whole creation is on tiptoe to see the wonderful sight of the sons of God coming into their own" (Romans 8:19 PNT).

Break up into small groups of two or three and share examples of how and where you see the gifts of the Spirit being recaptured by believers, with a focus on the fruits that are coming forth. Come back together as a large group and have one person from each group share your examples. Once everyone has shared, focus on the bigger picture of how God is moving to advance His Kingdom today.

PRAYER

Father, we thank You that we no longer need to live in bondage because Jesus has freed us from sin, making us servants of righteousness who eagerly await His final coming in glory. In this time between His first and second coming, we thank You for giving us the precious gift of the Holy Spirit, to empower us for the work of the Kingdom. We thank You that the Spirit is there for the asking, in generous measure, and that we, Your beloved sons and daughters, are coming into the fullness of who

You created us to be—Your people, walking in Your love and authority.

WEEKLY READING ASSIGNMENT

Read Chapter 14 and the Conclusion in *Authority to Heal* and be sure to complete your study guide assignments for the week.

A NEW PENTECOST

I believe God is going to breathe upon His whole
Church, across all denominational lines, awakening
all of us to His power and authority, and bringing
unity to the body—an ecumenism (unity) of the
Spirit rather than doctrinal ecumenism (unity). I
believe that the recovery of the gifts of the Spirit,
and the authority this gives to all believers are so
important to the heart of God for His Church that
He is going to cause both Protestants and Catholics
to pray for a new Pentecost, one in which the Church
will awaken afresh to the importance of the recovery
of the gifts. Because, without His presence and His
power and His authority—apart from signs and
wonders and the gifts of the Holy Spirit—many
more of those who don't know Him will not be
awakened to His truth. When so much has been
made available to the Church, why should we settle
for less? Jesus' authority to heal can be restored in
this generation, and for all the generations to come.

*Awake, O sleeper, and arise from the dead,
and Christ will shine on you. Look carefully*

then how you walk, not as unwise but as wise,
making the best use of the time, because the
days are evil. Therefore do not be foolish, but
understand what the will of the Lord is.
—EPHESIANS 5:14-17 ESV

SESSION 7 SUMMARY

Many today see a westernized Church that has fallen asleep to the fullness of the gospel of Jesus Christ, with methods of evangelism limited to debate and argument rather than augmented by God's gracelets of healing and working of miracles.

The Church of God and of our Lord Jesus Christ, in all its many streams, needs a restoration of all of the early gifts. But this restoration will not come without effort. We must be willing to wrestle against years of tradition and theology that have changed the makeup of the Church; wrestle against those who have confused the Church's understanding of itself. We must wrestle to awaken the sleeping Church in the West if we are to experience the fullness of the gospel in all the world.

We must press in for a new Pentecost, understanding that the devil fears our God-given power and authority to bring heaven to earth. He has worked hard to distract us from this by keeping us focused on a partial gospel that focuses on heaven and forgiveness, hoping we will not notice the present reality of our authority.

DISCUSSION QUESTIONS

Others, like seed sown on good soil, hear the word, accept it, and produce a crop—thirty, sixty or even a hundred times what was sown (Mark 4:20).

Reflect on Mark 4:20, taking note of the type of ground seed needs to fall on in order to yield a rich harvest. In this parable, all the seeds are the same; it is the type of ground that they fall upon that determines the harvest, and so it is with us. God will sow His seeds in our hearts and some will graciously receive them and allow them to grow into a plentiful harvest, while others will not so graciously receive them and as a result the harvest will be less or not at all.

1. What type of ground have the seeds of God found in your heart?

2. In Ephesians 5:14, Paul says, "Awake, O sleeper, and arise from the dead and Christ will shine on you." What is Paul saying in this verse? Why are we asleep, dead?

3. In the first paragraph in the Conclusion of *Authority to Heal*, Randy points out that our methods of evangelism are so often limited to debate and argument rather than being augmented by God's gracelets of healing and working of miracles. How do you feel about this statement that apologetics alone does not advance the Kingdom of God?

4. Randy points out that Satan and his demonic philosophies have been used to try and stop the fulfillment of Jesus' prayer—"Thy Kingdom come, thy will be done, on earth as it is in heaven." Do you see it this way also or do you disagree, and if so, why?

GROUP ACTIVATION

The first Pentecost resulted in the phenomenal growth of the early Church. Break up into groups of three or four and take time to reflect on what a second Pentecost would look like today, in the twenty-first century, allowing a reasonable amount of time for discussion. Then come back together and have someone from each group share what your group came up with. Once everyone has shared, come before the Lord as a group and pray, asking God for a new Pentecost in your heart and for the Church.

PRAYER

O Father, we cry out for You to rise up now, stretching forth Your Spirit over us in demonstrations of power and authority, so that we may partner with You to bring Your Kingdom to bear on the Kingdom of this world until all have heard the good news of the Kingdom of God.

WEEKLY READING ASSIGNMENT

Read the Conclusion in *Authority to Heal* and be sure to complete your study guide assignments for this week.

GOD WANTS TO USE YOU

God is looking for people through whom He can show Himself strong. He needs committed believers who are totally surrendered and yielded to His will—ones who are so hungry for God that they are willing to "go anywhere and do anything" if God will just use them.

"For the eyes of the Lord range throughout
the earth to strengthen those whose
hearts are fully committed to Him"
—2 CHRONICLES 16:9

SESSION 8 SUMMARY

In a number of Randy's books[1] he has shared how he experienced failure and rejection and yet he was so hungry for a deeper relationship with God and to be used by God that he persisted even in the face of great opposition. Although some said Randy would never be used by God, Scripture does not agree with them. God will use anyone He chooses, regardless of the opinions of man, because God knows the heart. He knows who really hungers and thirsts for righteousness for His name's sake.

If you recall from the story of the Samaritan woman at the well, she was not a well-respected person in her community, and yet that didn't seem to matter to God. He saw the brokenness and hunger in her heart and used her to bring her entire village and the surrounding region to Jesus. God is not looking for perfect vessels. If we let Him, He will take our "old wineskins" and make us new so that we can carry the good news.

DISCUSSION QUESTIONS:

Reflect on John 4:4-26, the story of Jesus' encounter with the Samaritan woman at the well. Notice that Scripture says that it was about the sixth hour when Jesus sat down by the well. It was an odd time of day for a woman to come alone to the well. Normally women of that day and time and place would come early in the morning to draw the water they would need for their daily tasks, and they would typically come together. But this woman had come alone, later in the day. Perhaps, because she was an outcast in her village, she avoided those times of day when the other women would be there.

This session is designed to take you through a study of Scriptures that provide ample evidence that God will use anyone He chooses, even you or me, even when we have fallen or failed, or just have no particularly impressive credentials in the eyes of the world.

1. Have you ever felt like an outcast in some way, like God would never use you for ministry? How do you think God sees you?

2. What does God see in your heart in terms of passion for Him and desperation to be used by Him?

3. In Second Chronicles 16:9, the Greek translation for the word *range* means to look intently. How would it feel to you if you realized God was looking intently and picked you out from the crowd?

4. In your own words, describe what it means to be "desperate" for God.

5. In verse 9 of John 4, in response to Jesus asking her for a drink of water, the Samaritan women reminds Him that she is "unclean." Jesus' response is to ignore her concern over her worldly status because He is more concerned with her eternal status. How would you respond if Jesus ignored all those things you think disqualify you and offered Himself anyway? (Hint: Isn't that what He did on the cross?)

6. Notice in verse 26 of John 4 how the Samaritan woman received the truth of who Jesus was because He saw directly into her heart. He saw her brokenness and her hunger to find that thing that would satisfy her heart. She had not found it in five husbands or her current boyfriend. But when she encountered Jesus and He spoke directly to her heart, she found what she had been looking for all along. She wasn't all "cleaned up" and "fit" for ministry, but her testimony carried the authority of the One she had encountered. God chose to use her in spite of her brokenness. How has God used you in spite of your brokenness?

GROUP ACTIVATION

Break up into small groups and allow a few minutes for each person to share how they feel they are disqualified and how they would like to be used by God even thought they are not "qualified." (At this point hopefully everyone feels very "safe" in their small groups.) Invite everyone to be as open and honest as they can about their disqualifications and how they would like to be used by God. Once everyone has had a few moments to share, go around the group and take time to pray for each person, asking God to respond to the deep desires of that person's heart to be used by Him (God).

PRAYER

O, Father, You knew each one of us before the foundations of the world, before we were formed in our mother's womb. You have loved us with an everlasting love through Your Son, Jesus Christ. Take us now, with our imperfections and failings, and make us into Your new wineskins. We are lost without You, desperate for You. We cannot accomplish Your will outside of Your power and authority. You are our heart's true home, the One we have been longing for. Pick us out of the crowd. Hear our cries—"Take me, pick me! Choose me! Use me!" You are the pearl of great price and we will go anywhere, do anything for You. Amen.

NOTE

1. *Lighting Fires, Open Heaven* and *Are You Thirsty?*

WATCH GOD ACCOMPLISH THE MIRACULOUS

THROUGH YOU.

LEARN FROM DR. RANDY CLARK!

Every Christian has been sent and empowered by Jesus to heal the sick. The problem is that many of us don't know how to practically complete this task.

In the *Power to Heal* curriculum, international evangelist, teacher, and apostolic voice, Dr. Randy Clark, shares eight practical, Bible-based tools that will help you start praying for the sick and see them supernaturally healed!

 Destiny Image  Destiny Image is a division of Nori Media Group. NMG

THE HOLY SPIRIT
WANTS TO WORK THROUGH YOU!

MANY CHRISTIANS HAVE EMBRACED THE DECEPTION THAT THE HOLY SPIRIT IS NO LONGER AT WORK.

But Dr. Randy Clark, President and Founder of Global Awakening, has been an *eyewitness* to the miraculous work of the Holy Spirit and a *key participant* in watching Him powerfully transform lives throughout the world. In this easy-to-read guide, he equips believers to understand and walk in the power of the Spirit every day.

- Discover the gifts of the Holy Spirit that are available to you.
- Recognize an authentic move of God in your church, community, & life.
- Understand how miracles, signs, and wonders play a key role evangelism.

FULFILL YOUR DESTINY! UNLOCK THE POWER OF THE HOLY SPIRIT IN YOUR LIFE.

 Destiny Image is a division of Nori Media Group.

Christian Prophetic
CERTIFICATION PROGRAM

We are happy to announce the launch of the
**Christian Prophetic Certification Program
(CPCP).**

CPCP will teach students how to recognize the gift of prophecy in
their own life, allowing them to better recognize communications
from the Holy Spirit.

Students will gain a truly Biblical perspective on the prophetic both
from the Old and New Testaments. They will also learn about the
history of prophesy within the church, its benefits and the ways in
which it went off track.

**Courses are available online
and can be taken anywhere at any time.**

Check out our website for more details at
propheticcertification.com

JOIN US!

globalawakening

lighting fires • building bridges • casting vision

Based in Mechanicsburg, PA, the Apostolic Network of Global Awakening (ANGA) is a teaching, healing and impartation ministry with a heart for the nations. Founded in 1994 by Randy Clark after his involvement with the Toronto Airport Christian Fellowship revival, the ministry exists to fulfill the biblical commissions of Jesus:

> As you go preach, saying the Kingdom of heaven is at hand. Heal the sick, cleanse the lepers, raise the dead, cast out demons. Freely you have received, freely give (Matthew 10:7-8).

> Therefore go and make disciples of all nations, baptizing them in the name of the Father and of the Son and of the Holy Spirit, and teaching them to obey everything I have commanded you. And surely I am with you always, to the very end of the age (Matthew 28:19-20).

Through the formation of ANGA, International Ministry Trips (IMT), the Schools of Healing and Impartation and the Global School of Supernatural Ministry, Global Awakening offers training, conferences, humanitarian aid, and ministry trips in an effort to raise up a company of men and women who will facilitate revival among the nation's leaders. By providing an assortment of international training opportunities, the ministry works in accordance with the revelation to the Apostle Paul regarding the purpose of the five fold ministries:

> It was He who gave some to be apostles, some to be prophets, some to be evangelists, and some to be pastors and teachers, to prepare God's people for works of service, so that the body of Christ may be built up until we all reach unity in the faith and in the knowledge of the Son of God and become mature, attaining to the whole measure of the fullness of Christ (Ephesians 4:11-13).

Led by Rev. Randy Clark, the ministry has visited over 36 countries and continues to travel extensively to bring hope, healing, and power to the nations.

globalawakening.com

f ▶ 𝕐 ⊡ ≫